Jean Baptiste Pointe du Sable

⊢ FATHER OF ⊢

CHICAGO

Debra Lucas

CONTENTS

Rigby

A Harcourt Achieve Imprint

www.Rigby.com
1-800-531-5015

CHAPTER 1

Big and Busy

Chicago, Illinois, is one of the biggest and busiest cities in the United States. It is filled with museums, restaurants, zoos, houses, apartment buildings, and stores. The city has some of the world's tallest buildings, two professional baseball teams, the world's busiest airport, and nearly three million people—but it wasn't always so big. Back in 1779, the United States was only three years old, and the state of Illinois didn't even exist. The place that would one day become Chicago was in the middle of a huge wilderness that the new United States would soon call the Northwest Territory.

Before 1779 the only people who lived near the place we now call Chicago were American Indians known as the Potawatomis, the Ottawas, and the Winnebagos. But that year, an outsider came into the area and built a lonely cabin near the shore of Lake Michigan, on the north bank of a small river. This single cabin was the first step in the making of a huge city.

Jean Baptiste Pointe du Sable came with his wife to the shore of Lake Michigan to work and make a home for

Long before it was lined with tall buildings, the shore of Lake Michigan was a wilderness.

them both. Du Sable recognized that the southern end of Lake Michigan would soon be an important crossroads for travel and trade among American settlers, American Indians, and Europeans. His new cabin would be in the perfect spot to help everyone exchange their goods.

But who was Jean Baptiste Pointe du Sable, and where did he come from? What parts of his character made him just the right person to start one of the world's greatest cities? Let's see why Jean du Sable is considered the father of Chicago.

Historians are people who try to find out facts about people and events from long ago. Sometimes historians only have to go to libraries or offices where records are kept and look up information printed in books or on old papers and letters. But often there are no good records from the past. In those cases, historians have to piece together little bits of information from different places and different times. Sometimes these scraps of information don't agree with each other, and historians have to decide which information they think is most likely to be true.

This has been the case with the story of Jean Baptiste Pointe du Sable. Historians have good information about his life in the area around present-day Chicago, and they know more facts about his later life. But they have had to depend on many different little pieces of information, including some tales and legends, to put together a more complete picture of his early life.

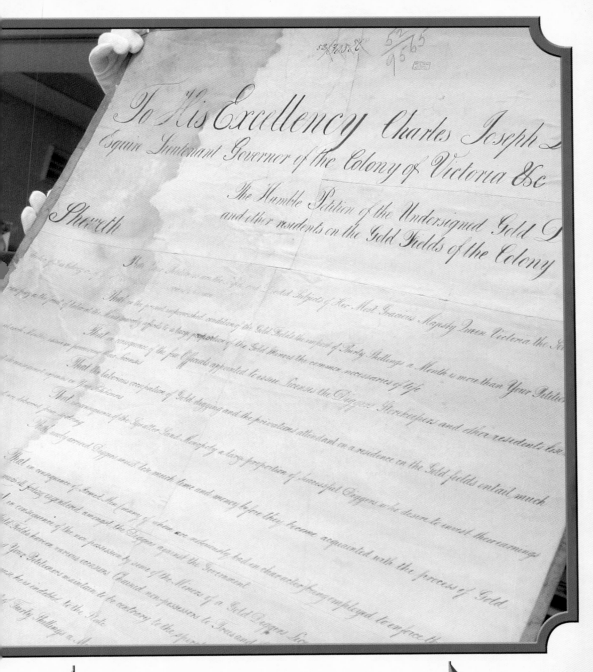

To His Excellency Charles Joseph

Esquire Lieutenant Governor of the Colony of Victoria &c

The Humble Petition of the Undersigned Gold D
and other residents on the Gold Fields of the Colony

Sheweth

Historians often study very old letters and papers.

CHAPTER 2

Leaving Home

Jean Baptiste Pointe du Sable was born around the middle of the 18th century. There are no certain records of his exact birth date, but historians think that he was born sometime around 1745. Some stories about du Sable say that he was born a slave somewhere in the southern part of the present United States, perhaps near New Orleans. But most historians believe he was born in what is now the island nation of Haiti, in the Caribbean Sea.

Islands of the Caribbean Sea

Du Sable's mother and other slaves grew and harvested sugar cane on many Caribbean islands.

Du Sable's father was a French sailor, and his mother was an African slave who had been brought to the island to grow and harvest sugar cane on a **plantation**. It is not clear whether the mother was ever set free. Historians believe that du Sable's father was at sea much of the time when du Sable was a boy. One common legend about du Sable's life says that around 1763 or 1764, Spanish pirates attacked the area around du Sable's home, and that while his mother died in the attack, his father was able to rescue young du Sable and take him on a ship to France. Du Sable would never return to the place of his birth.

Some historians think that du Sable never had any formal education. Others, however, say that du Sable went to school in France and learned reading, writing, arithmetic, and geography.

During his years in Haiti and on his voyage to France, he also learned to love the sea, and du Sable begged his father to allow him to become a sailor. According to the story, du Sable's father at first only let him work to make repairs on ships that were docked in port, but after a couple of years, his father agreed to find a place for du Sable as a sailor aboard one of his ships.

The legends say that sometime in 1765, when du Sable was about twenty years old, he and his father set sail for the Caribbean Sea aboard a ship called the *Suzanne*. After sailing for several weeks, the ship ran into a huge storm at sea. The *Suzanne* was tossed around by the storm, and it eventually broke apart and sank.

Du Sable worked on a ship similar to this one. The life of a sailor in the 1700s was both dangerous and exciting.

Spanish New Orleans was a dangerous place for young du Sable.

Some members of the crew didn't make it to shore, and records don't show what happened to the boy's father. Du Sable, however, was pulled from the sea and brought safely to the port of New Orleans, at the mouth of the great Mississippi River, in what is now the U.S. state of Louisiana.

New Orleans had begun as a French colony and port in the early 1700s, but in 1765 it was under Spanish control. As the son of a French sailor, du Sable was a free man. But because he was also the son of an African woman who had been a slave, he believed that he was in danger in Spanish New Orleans. He wouldn't be able to prove to Spanish officials that he was free, and he feared being sold into slavery.

The Mississippi River

- St. Louis

Mississippi River

New Orleans •

Gulf of Mexico

● French settlements visted by du Sable

— Modern state boundry lines

The Mississippi River flowed through a wilderness when Jean Baptiste Pointe du Sable first travelled on it.

At this time, many free men and women of African descent lived in New Orleans, and they helped du Sable by leading him to some French **missionaries** who fed him and hid him from the Spanish. While working for the missionaries, he met and befriended an American Indian man from the Choctaw people who spoke often of traveling north, up the Mississippi River, to make a living trading with other American Indians.

Du Sable liked the idea of making a life for himself in a new land. Together, he and his Choctaw friend built a flat-bottomed boat, gathered the supplies they needed, and set sail northward along the great river.

CHAPTER 3

Travels in a New World

After weeks of sailing against the Mississippi's strong current, the two men arrived in the settlement of St. Louis, at the place where the Mississippi and Missouri rivers come together. St. Louis was another town built by the French. Here, hundreds of European, American, and American Indian hunters and traders exchanged goods for money and supplies.

The busy town excited du Sable, and he decided that he would make his living as a trader, too. However, du Sable also realized that the people who gained the most from trade were the ones who ran the trading posts, and there were already several posts in St. Louis. There might not be enough business to support a new one. So he decided to travel farther north to set up his own trading post.

Many people in du Sable's time made a living trading furs and other goods.

Stories say that one day while traveling farther upriver, du Sable and his Choctaw friend found themselves surrounded by American Indian canoes. The people in the canoes were American Indian Ottawas, and they guided du Sable and his friend to the riverbank. Once ashore, the Ottawas led the two men to a village and into a large house made of logs, branches, and tree bark.

Du Sable and his companion waited, and then a quiet, important-looking man entered. The man greeted du Sable and his friend in a language neither of them could understand. Du Sable spoke to his friend in French, and when the important-looking man heard these words, he smiled. He then greeted du Sable again in French, the language the man had learned while hunting and trading with French explorers many years before. The man was Pontiac, chief of the Ottawa people.

Pontiac was a famous leader of the Ottawa people.

Du Sable told the chief that he and his friend had come in peace to the land of the Ottawas. He assured the chief that he had great respect for the land and did not wish to take it away from Pontiac's people. In the past, the chief had met many men who lied to him and proved that they couldn't be trusted. But Pontiac believed du Sable, and over time, the two men became friends.

Jean Baptiste Pointe du Sable lived among the Ottawa people for almost two years. The American Indians taught him about the wilderness. They also taught him how to ride a horse, how to track animals, how to hunt, and how to trap animals for their valuable fur. One spring day, du Sable realized that it was time to head out again on his own. His friends, the Ottawa people, wished him luck.

Pontiac's people lived in houses much like the ones in this Mandan village.

CHAPTER 4

The Fur Trade

In 1768 the United States had not yet become an independent nation. The country was still under British rule, and because du Sable was French, he had to get permission from the British government to work in the region as a fur trader. Du Sable received permission and went into business near the area where the Mississippi and Illinois rivers meet.

Fur traders played an important role in the history of North America. Fine fur was very fashionable in the cities of Europe, and there were large numbers of fur-bearing animals in the wilderness that covered most of North America. Many early European settlers as well as American Indians made their living by trapping or hunting animals and selling their fur. They would take the furs to a trading post and exchange them for supplies like metal tools, new clothing, gunpowder, and other manufactured goods. Sometimes they exchanged furs, or pelts, for small amounts of money.

Items Traded by American Indian, American, and European Fur Trappers

Beaver Furs Traded		Items Received	
QUANTITY	ITEM	QUANTITY	ITEM
2	Furs	4	Shirts
3	Furs	1	Large Coat
4	Furs	8 pounds	Gunpowder
6	Furs	1	Barrel of Corn
6	Furs	1	Blanket

The people who ran the trading posts sold the furs to manufacturers in Europe. Many people in North America and in Europe used the furs to make fine coats, boots, blankets, and fancy hats. The fur of beavers was used to make a valuable, waterproof felt for very expensive hats. The white fur of a small, weasel-like animal called an ermine was used to make robes for kings, queens, and other members of royal families.

The people who ran the trading posts received lots of money for the furs, and many of them made a very good living. Some became wealthy enough to build mills that ground wheat and corn into flour and meal. These people also often owned farms and bakeries, and they offered food for the hunters and trappers to eat.

A hat made out of beaver fur

The black-tipped white fur on this queen's robe is from an ermine.

Fur traders doing business in the 1700s

There were almost no towns or cities to visit in the wilderness, so the trading posts often served as banks and post offices as well as general stores, restaurants, and meeting places.

Jean Baptiste Pointe du Sable began his career in the wilderness by tracking and trapping for furs near present-day Peoria, Illinois. He traded some of the furs for the supplies he needed to survive, and the rest he exchanged for money. He saved his money for the day he would build his own trading post. He traveled all over much of the area known as the Midwest, including what are now the states of Illinois, Indiana, Wisconsin, and Michigan. Du Sable befriended several American Indian groups in the area, and he formed close bonds with members of the Potawatomi people.

An artist traveling in the Midwest in the 1830s painted this picture of a Potawatomi warrior.

Du Sable worked closely with American Indians, helping them when he could. The Potawatomi people trusted him and showed him where and how to trap more animals and how to find his way around the region.

In order to make their bond with du Sable even stronger, the Potawatomis arranged for him to marry a young woman from their group. The woman's Potawatomi name was Kittihawa, but du Sable called her Catherine. Du Sable and his wife lived together for many years and had two children, Suzanne and Jean Baptiste.

A Native American wedding

CHAPTER 5

Prisoner!

The fur trade required that a trapper move to new areas, because if the person stayed too long in one place, there would be few animals left to trap, and the trapper could no longer make a living. By about 1777, Jean Baptiste Pointe du Sable and his family had moved north and east, to a spot near what is now Michigan City, Indiana. Du Sable needed to look after his family, so he couldn't go off by himself into the wilderness any longer. He took a job running a trading post belonging to another Frenchman named Pierre Durand.

The year before, in 1776, the American colonists had decided to become an independent nation and had gone to war against the king of England and his army. The area around Durand's trading post was still under the control of British soldiers. The British discovered that Pierre Durand was selling supplies to American soldiers. And because du Sable worked for Durand, the British arrested du Sable for being too friendly with Americans. The British sent du Sable to jail at what became Fort Mackinac, in Michigan, and kept him there for more than one year.

While he was a prisoner at Fort Mackinac, du Sable worried about his family. How would they survive without him? Once again, the American Indians helped. The Chippewa people asked the British to release du Sable, and he was **reunited** with his family.

Today, Fort Mackinac is a tourist spot. Visitors can see what life was like during the time Jean Baptiste Pointe du Sable was a prisoner here.

Du Sable and his family returned to the area of their first home, near Peoria. They were anxious to move away from the soldiers and the war, and they needed some time to gather their money and supplies. After taking a few months to prepare, in 1779 du Sable moved to the southwest shore of Lake Michigan, to the north bank of the mouth of a small river. There he built a large cabin, created a small farm, and set up his own trading post. Once business was going well, he sent for his wife and children to join him.

This is one artist's idea of the way du Sable's cabin on Lake Michigan might have looked.

The Midwest

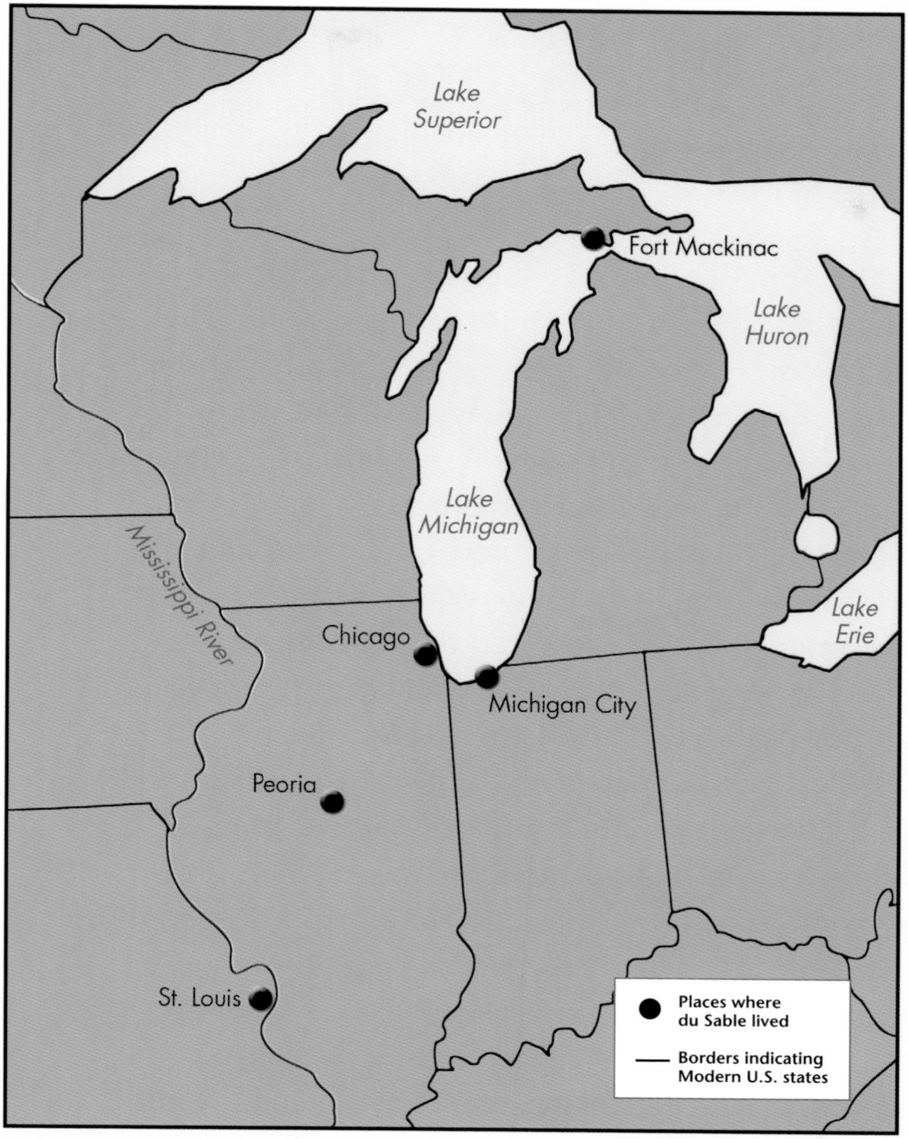

Lake Superior

Fort Mackinac

Lake Huron

Lake Michigan

Mississippi River

Chicago

Michigan City

Lake Erie

Peoria

St. Louis

● Places where du Sable lived

— Borders indicating Modern U.S. states

CHAPTER 6

Eschikagou

The American Indians, who were the only people besides du Sable and his family to live near his new trading post, called the river Eschikagou, which meant "place of bad smells." No one is really sure why the river was given this name. It might have been because of the swamp near the river's mouth. Wild onions were also known to grow in the area, and they have a strong smell, too. Whatever the source of the name, du Sable recognized that this spot was a perfect location for trading with American, European, and American Indians trappers and fur traders.

His cabin was quite large for the times. It had five comfortable rooms with nice furniture. Some historians claim that du Sable had several barns for hay and animals, a mill for grinding grain, a bakery, a dairy for milk and cheese, and a large smokehouse for preserving meat. People from far away knew of du Sable's post at Eschikagou, and many hunters, trappers, and traders of all cultural backgrounds came to trade there.

The inside of du Sable's home at Eschikagou may have looked something like this.

Historians believe that du Sable could speak many languages, and that this was one of the reasons his trading post was such a success. He had spoken French from childhood. He learned Spanish and English when he lived in New Orleans and St. Louis. And in the many years he spent with his wife and other American Indians, he learned several of their languages as well. Du Sable could arrange trade deals between people from different cultural backgrounds who had trouble understanding each other, and so he gained the trust and respect of many people.

The trading post continued to be a success for many years. The first child born in what would become Chicago was du Sable's granddaughter, Eulalie. The first wedding, the first election, and the first law court in Chicago were all held at his trading post.

But not everything went well for Jean Baptiste Pointe du Sable. A few years after his family had joined him at Eschikagou, the British built a small fort across the river from du Sable's cabin. From time to time, du Sable had trouble with the British soldiers, until they lost their war with the Americans and left the area.

Historians are not certain about what happened next. They know that sometime shortly after 1790, du Sable's wife died. They also believe that one of his children died around this time, but two different stories are told. One says that his daughter died and that du Sable continued to run the trading post with his son. The other version says that du Sable's son died and his daughter was married at the trading post. Whichever version is true, historians are fairly sure that du Sable continued to live at Eschikagou with one of his children for several more years.

In 1795 the new United States government made an agreement with the American Indians living near du Sable's trading post that would allow the U.S. Army to build a fort on the land across the river, near the old British fort. As the U.S. soldiers arrived, settlers from the United States began to follow them into the area. Soon the settlers were taking up land to build farms, and the American Indians were forced to move farther west.

In 1800 Jean Baptiste Pointe du Sable sold his trading post. He then moved to a farm near St. Charles, in the Missouri Territory, with his surviving child.

Parts of St. Charles, Missouri, still look much as they did when Jean Baptiste Pointe du Sable lived there.

Once again, historians are not really certain just why du Sable left Eschikagou. Perhaps as he got older, it became too hard for him to run the trading post without the help of his wife and both children. Another reason may be that many of the soldiers and settlers that came into the area began to treat du Sable unfairly because he was of African and French descent.

Whatever his reasons for leaving, it is certain that du Sable left behind the first important building blocks of a fast-growing new settlement. The soldiers had finished building their new fort by 1803, naming it Fort Dearborn. A town quickly grew up around the fort, and soon it was the largest town in the entire Midwest. People who lived there changed the spelling of Eschikagou to "Chicago."

Du Sable lived peacefully with his child and grandchild on a farm near St. Charles until 1818. That year, at age 73, he died in his sleep and was buried in Borromeo Cemetery.

Jean Baptiste Pointe du Sable led a life of adventure, exploration, and achievement. He sought only to make a living for himself and his family, but in doing so, he **founded** one of the greatest cities in the world.

An artist's view of old Fort Dearborn

CHAPTER 7

Chicago Grows Up

The Fort Dearborn settlement continued to **prosper**. By 1812, most people there had forgotten the man who built the first cabin on the Chicago River. More than 100 people lived in the village besides the soldiers who guarded the fort. But that year, the British decided to try to take back the land they had lost to the American colonists. Another war began, and the U.S. government thought it would be better if the soldiers at Fort Dearborn returned to the East to help with the fighting.

When the soldiers left, the settlers in the area feared that the American Indians they had pushed out earlier would come and try to get their land back. They **abandoned** their settlement and ran away. The American Indians did return, and they burned down Fort Dearborn and the surrounding buildings. Only a handful of settlers remained in the area.

The Americans won the second war against the British in 1814, and by 1816 the U.S. government decided that it would be a good idea to rebuild Fort Dearborn and resettle the area. American settlers returned and rebuilt the town started by Jean Baptiste Pointe du Sable.

Soldiers and settlers rebuilt Fort Dearborn
after it was burned, and the town grew quickly.
By 1830 more than three thousand people
lived there.

Again many American Indians were forced to move to new lands farther west. Some were forced to leave the Midwest altogether and settled in areas now in present-day Kansas and Oklahoma. The U.S. government wanted to make room for more farms and settlements.

Thousands of American settlers came to Fort Dearborn to help build the new city. Although most of these settlers spoke English, they came from many different European cultural backgrounds and spoke many different languages. Very few of these new settlers thought much about the unfairness to the American Indians who had lived in the Chicago area for hundreds of years.

Chicago in the early 1800s looked very different from both Eschikagou and present-day Chicago.

◀ **A view of Chicago in the 1840s** ▶

Du Sable had been right about Chicago's location. It was in the perfect place to become the center of trade among people from every direction. Goods and materials could be sailed down Lake Michigan from the north to the port at the mouth of the Chicago River. **Canals** and rivers would connect the town to the great Mississippi River, where those goods and materials could be shipped to the Gulf of Mexico, and from there, around the world.

Through the 1800s, the population of Chicago grew at a faster rate than the population of the whole United States. Most of the thousands of new buildings that went up in Chicago to house these people were made of wood, however, and in 1871, a huge fire destroyed a large part of the city. But people living in Chicago would not let the disaster stop the growth of the city. Many famous building designers came to Chicago to help the city rebuild itself out of steel and brick. The city of Chicago was rebuilt and grew even more.

The world's first **skyscraper** was built in Chicago in 1889. The tallest building in the United States, the Sears Tower, was built there in 1973.

The people of Chicago rebuilt the city after the fire of 1871, and they kept on building.

Three of the four tallest buildings in the United States are in Chicago, and these three buildings are among the twenty tallest buildings in the world! Chicago's population jumped from less than 300,000 in the middle of the 1800s to more than 3,000,000 in the middle of the 1900s. No one in Eschikagou in 1779 could ever have imagined so many people living near their little trading post!

Growth of a City, Growth of a Nation

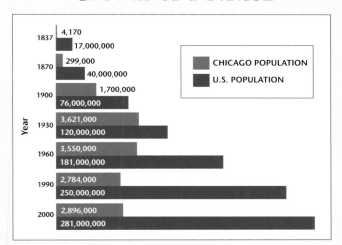

Year	CHICAGO POPULATION	U.S. POPULATION
1837	4,170	17,000,000
1870	299,000	40,000,000
1900	1,700,000	76,000,000
1930	3,621,000	120,000,000
1960	3,550,000	181,000,000
1990	2,784,000	250,000,000
2000	2,896,000	281,000,000

Between 1837 and 1930 Chicago grew to be one of the biggest cities in the United States.

CHAPTER 8

Honoring du Sable

But what about the French-African fur trader who built the first cabin on the shore of Lake Michigan? Had he been completely forgotten? On October 25, 1968, the city of Chicago and the state of Illinois officially recognized Jean Baptiste Pointe du Sable as the founder of Chicago. A postage stamp with his picture on it was released in 1987 as part of a series of stamps dedicated to African American history. And today, a **plaque** near the sidewalk of the Michigan Avenue Bridge over the Chicago River marks a spot close to the location of du Sable's cabin. If you walk past the Tribune Tower and the Wrigley Building, you will be standing in Jean du Sable's front yard, the site of the first home in Eschikagou—today's great city of Chicago.

Jean Baptiste Pointe du Sable appears on a 1987 U.S. postage stamp.

Today, Chicago's Wrigley Building and Tribune Tower mark the site of Jean Baptiste Pointe du Sable's 1779 trading post.

GLOSSARY

abandoned left

canals man-made rivers

founded started

missionaries people who try to teach their religion to people who do not believe in that religion

plantation large farm usually growing only one kind of crop

plaque special sign or label

prosper grow or succeed

reunited brought back together

skyscraper very tall building

INDEX